Pebble® Plus

Spokes

BIKE SAFETY
A Crash Course

BY LISA J. AMSTUTZ

Gail Saunders-Smith, PhD,
consulting editor

CAPSTONE PRESS
a capstone imprint

Pebble Plus is published by Capstone Press,
1710 Roe Crest Drive, North Mankato, Minnesota 56003.
www.capstonepub.com

Library of Congress Cataloging-in-Publication Data
Amstutz, Lisa J.
Bike safety: a crash course / by Lisa J. Amstutz.
pages cm.—(Pebble plus. spokes)
Includes bibliographical references and index.
Summary: "Full-color photos and simple text introduce the basics of bicycle safety"—Provided by publisher.
ISBN 978-1-4765-3965-2 (library binding)
ISBN 978-1-4765-6028-1 (ebook pdf)
1. Cycling—Safety measures—Juvenile literature. 2. Bicycles—Safety measures—Juvenile literature. I. Title.
GV1055.A67 2014
796.6028'9—dc23   2013031426

Editorial Credits
Jeni Wittrock, editor; Kyle Grenz, designer; Jennifer Walker, production specialist; Sarah Schuette, photo stylist;
Marcy Morin, photo scheduler

Photo Credits
Capstone Studio: Karon Dubke, 5, 7, 9; Corbis: Mika, 15; Glow Images: All Canada Photos/Henry Georgi, 17, Bridge/Corbis/
Holger Winkler/A.B., 11; iStockphotos: mo64, 19 (all); Shutterstock: Monkey Business Images, 21, spotmatik, cover, 13

Design Elements:
Shutterstock: filip robert, Kalmatsuy Tatyana

Note to Parents and Teachers

The Spokes set supports national science standards related to physical activities, recreation, and safety. This book describes and illustrates bicycle safety. The images support early readers in understanding the text. The repetition of words and phrases helps early readers learn new words. This book also introduces early readers to subject-specific vocabulary words, which are defined in the Glossary section. Early readers may need assistance to read some words and to use the Table of Contents, Glossary, Read More, Internet Sites, and Index sections of the book.

Printed in the United States of America in North Mankato, Minnesota.
012015   008670R

Table of Contents

Safety First

It's a perfect day for
a bike ride. The sun is out
and your friends are ready
to roll. But wait!
Think about safety first.

What to Wear

Bikers need the right gear.

A helmet protects your head.

Fasten the strap snugly

under your chin.

What you wear is important.

Bright colors make it easy to

be seen. Avoid loose clothing.

It might get caught in the

bike chain. Tie shoelaces tight.

Safety Check

If your bike isn't working right, it's not safe to ride. Always test your brakes. They should stop the wheels from turning. The tires should feel firm.

It's important to sit comfortably on your bike. Make sure your feet touch the pedals. The handlebars should be easy to reach.

Use Your Head

Bike paths and sidewalks are safe places to ride. Need to cross the street? Hop off your bike and walk across the crosswalk. Look both ways first.

When you ride, pay attention. Don't talk on a cell phone or wear headphones. Keep your hands on the handlebars and your feet on the pedals.

Stay Safe

Beep! Avoid getting in a crash. A horn or bell lets others know you are near. Use hand signals to show where you are headed.

left turn

stop

right turn

Tell an adult where you
are biking. Someone might
need to find you. Always
bike home before dark.
Have fun and ride safe!

Glossary

brake—a tool that slows down or stops a bike

crosswalk—a place where people can safely cross the street

handlebar—the part of a bicycle that the rider holds on to and uses to steer

hand signal—a special sign to show others that you plan to stop or turn

helmet—a hard hat that protects the head

sidewalk—a hard path that gives people a safe place to walk, run, or bike away from traffic

Read More

Hamilton, Robert M. *On a Bike.* Going Places. New York: Gareth Stevens Pub., 2012.

Herrington, Lisa M. *Bicycle Safety.* Rookie Read-About Safety. New York: Children's Press, 2013.

Maurer, Tracy Nelson. *Bicycle Riding.* Sports for Sprouts. Vero Beach, Fla.: Rourke Pub., 2011.

Internet Sites

FactHound offers a safe, fun way to find Internet sites related to this book. All of the sites on FactHound have been researched by our staff.

Here's all you do:

Visit *www.facthound.com*

Type in this code: 9781476539652

Super-cool stuff! Check out projects, games and lots more at **www.capstonekids.com**

Index

Word Count: 219
Grade: 1
Early-Intervention Level: 15